I0505580

The Mystics Coloring Book

Written By: Chantal Cash

Illustrated By: Chantal Cash

Contributions By:

Beatrice Cash, Jenny Atwell &

Alicia Lambson

The Mystics coloring book is for anyone who wants to explore their imagination through creative means. For best results please use colored pencils. For outlining I prefer to use sharpies or some other fine tip pen with an array of colors to enhance the lines; in addition some areas are indeed left to the imagination—some faint some strong.

I work daily in the imagination. I write stories; I make art and create scrapbooks as well. It is in my blood you could say. This book is special; it was motivated by an artist friend and some of the pieces were based on her edits; but all were based on my original work, edits and other intuitive insights to create this book.

Suggestions for a better coloring experience are as follows: Slip a piece of paper in between the pages as you color. Realize that it is a different type of paper than other books so do not use erasers too often as it could put small tears and worn spots into the image.

As a child I enjoyed coloring; but I wanted something fantastical and that would stimulate my imagination further and also help my artistic skills to grow. We all have a painter, or artist or skilled creator inside of ourselves. We are co-creators with Creation. Step into this magical realm. There are light codes, angelic symbols, digitalized versions of embroidery and much more presented in this fun and unique coloring book.

Please open your hearts to new things, new ideas and feelings. I tried to convey spiritual visions that I have seen, and through my art I have now transformed it for all of you. This is the perfect way to start a day or end a day; coloring in this book and opening your mind to the mystics dream.

Be open to receiving; be open to believing. Much love, and light and creativity—may it surround you and fill you up with joy and mirth.

## Dedication

This is dedicated to Alicia Lambson; a magical woman who beat her dis-ease. She was inspired to heal through creativity and guidance. She moved me to share my heart and our Art with the world. Blessings friend—may you light up the world! May you shine and continue to heal and help others.

## Alicia's Wings

My dear friend at all odds against her beat her illness. This is proof that you can too. She is a fighter, and a mother and a friend. She decided that her illness would not win and then as her healing continued she started to do art—this is one of the pieces she has donated to this amazing cause and illustrated book. Alicia has found her wings!

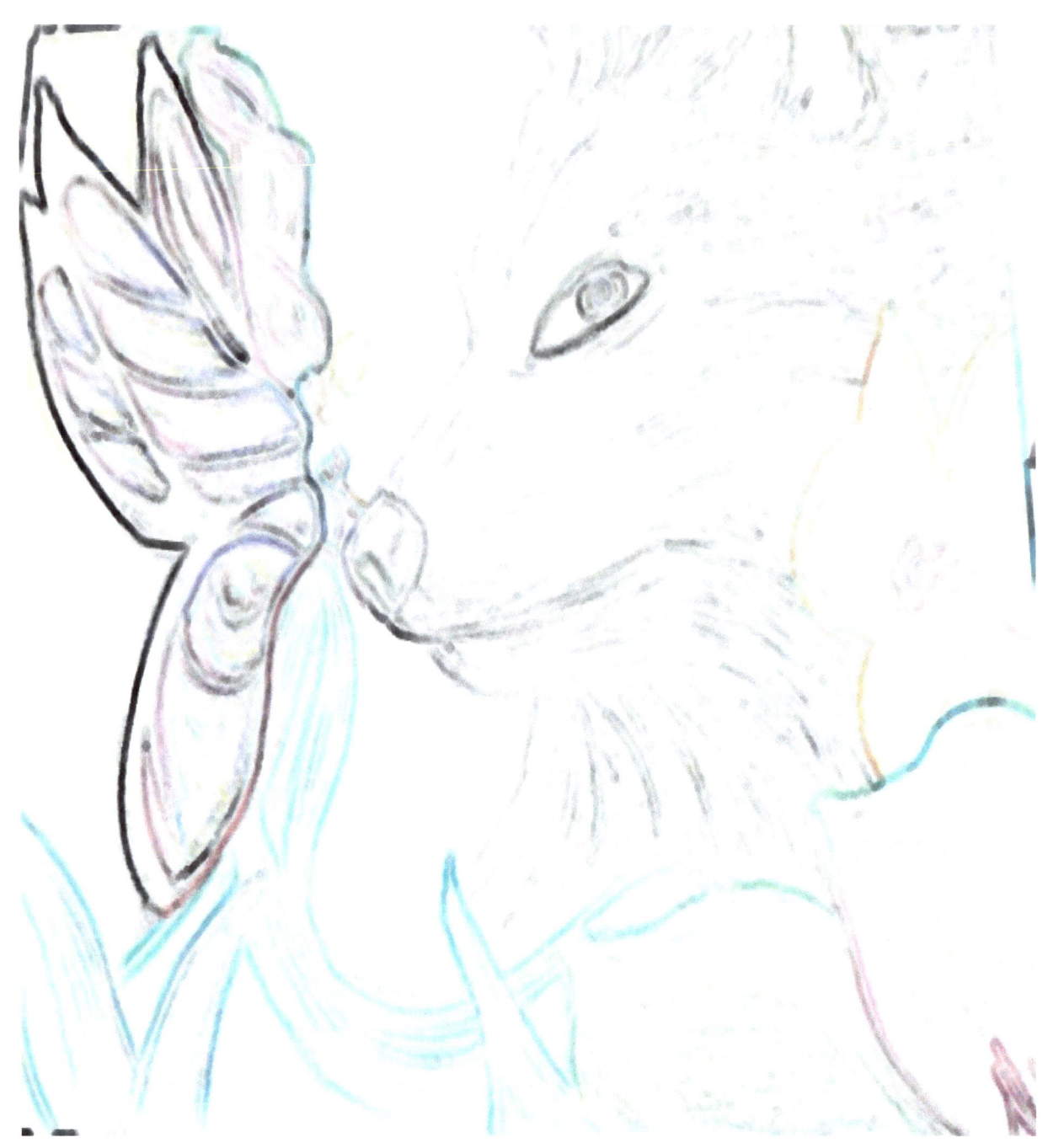

# The Eternal Lotus

This is the Eternal Lotus symbol. It was first drawn by Reiki Master Teacher Chantal Cash—this here is Jenny Atwell's re-creation of the original symbol. This is infinite the soul and its worthiness is something to be valued and guarded carefully. Those who have been hurt in love this symbol is for you. Focus on the colors that move your heart to emotional freedom.

# Kuan Yin

This is The Lady of Light and of the Lotus flower. It was a piece of art embroidered by Chantal and it was then re-edited by Jenny Atwell—this image shows her looking downward in an expression of grace. She sits atop the lotus and she creates peace with you as you attune to her loving and compassionate frequency.

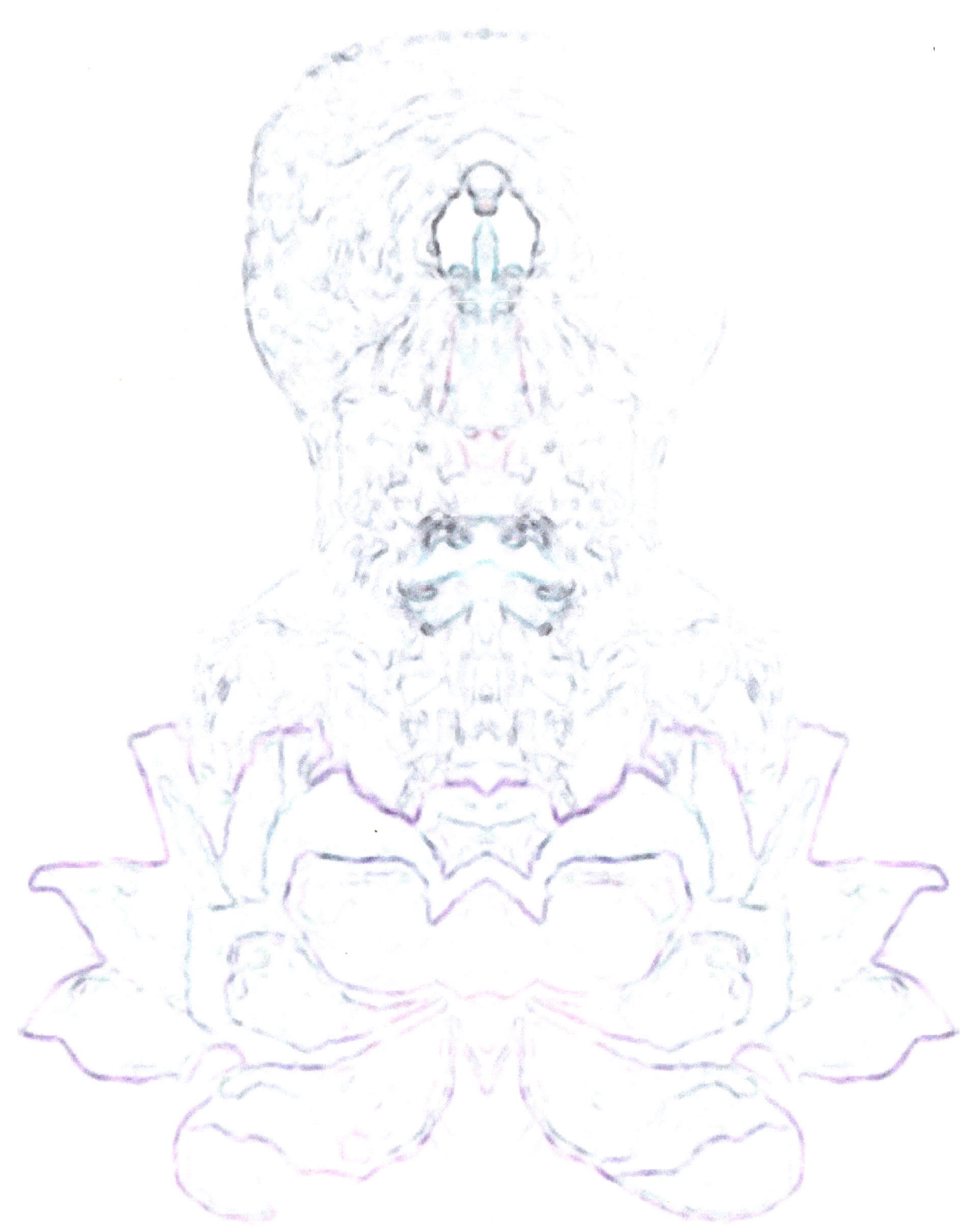

# The Shell

Based on the original symbol in the *Energy Symbols* book by Chantal Cash—this was painted and re-mastered and put into a format for coloring. It is based on the Fibonacci spiral and it is represented here as a shell on the beach. This is one of the most simplistic yet important symbols in the Universe. You will recognize it often in nature.

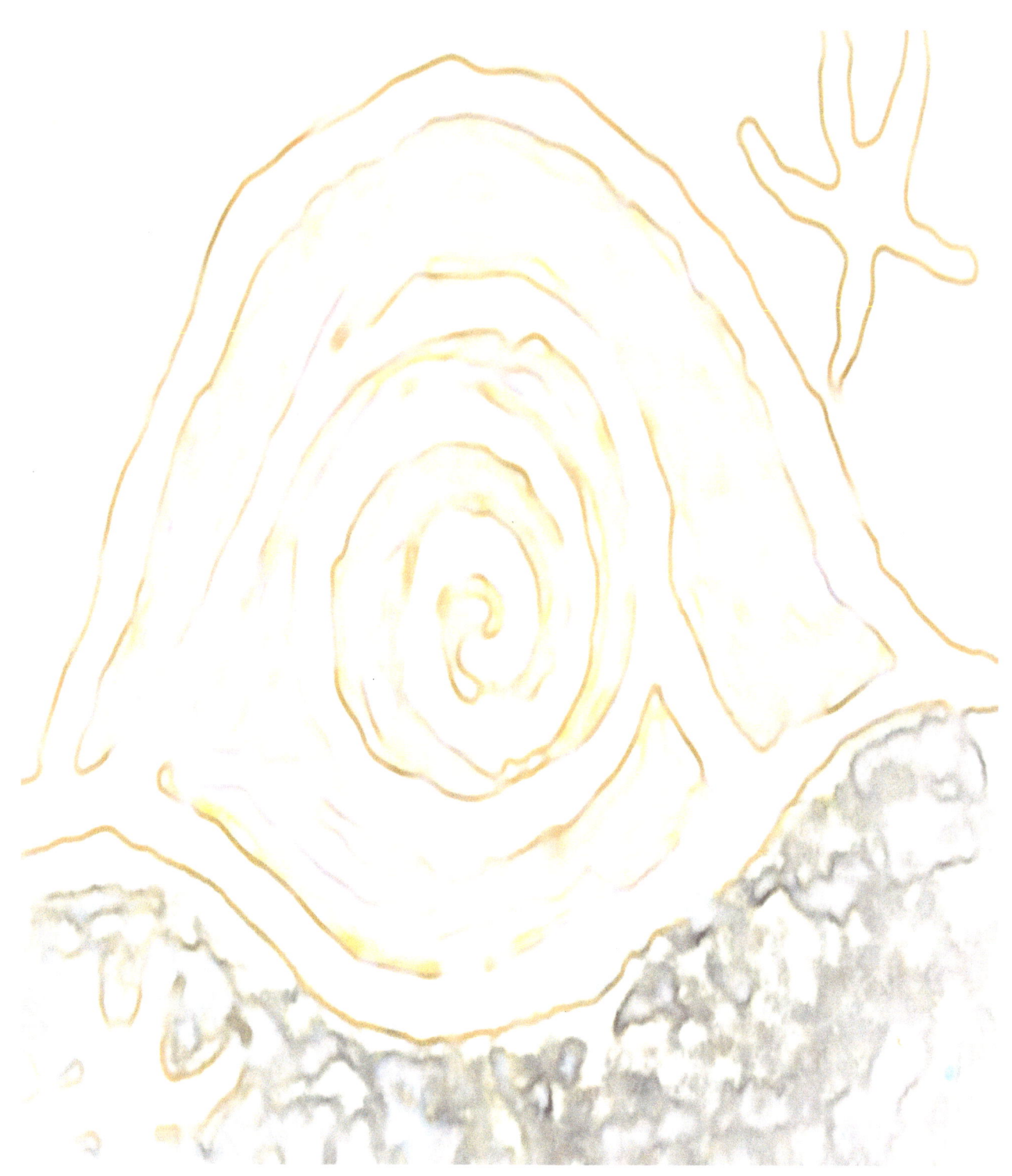

# The Fae Ground

This is a photograph of a fairy garden that the artist creates in the summer months. She has recreated the scene here for the delight of those who are inspired by fairies and the elemental realms. The Fox and the Fairy are both present here as they frolic in a play ground of wonder and curiosity.

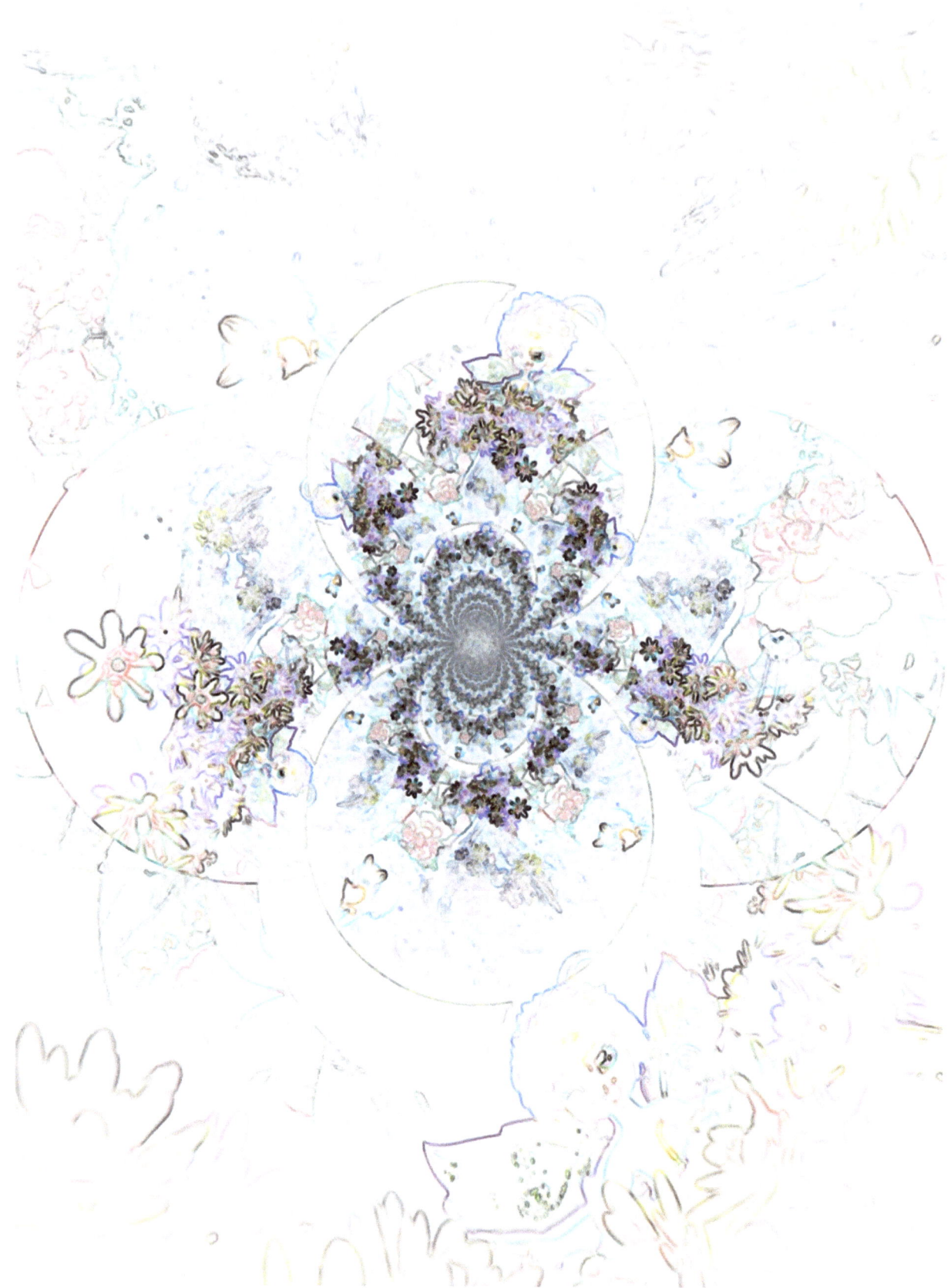

## The Dream of the Maiden

This is the dream of the Maiden; she is in a meditative state—she breathes life into all things; her breath is pure and she refreshes the soul. Her many fractals and higher selves are joyful at the peace in her heart—this is her enlightened dream state.

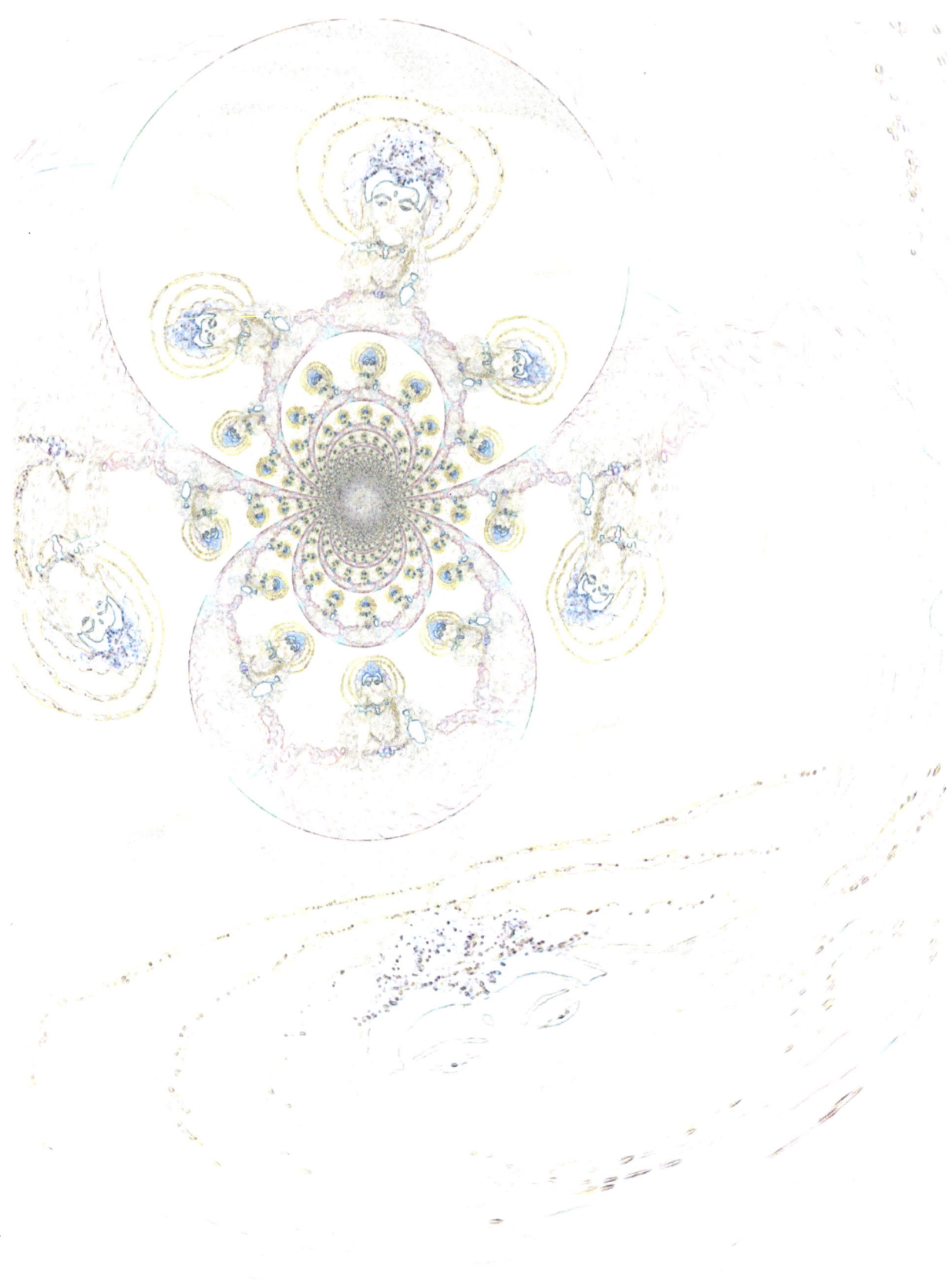

# The Moth

My daughter took a photo of a moth—this is the re-created art piece for those who enjoy the eyes of the moth. They often blend in with nature on the side of a house or a tree. They are small or large; seen and often unseen. This is the beauty of the hidden moth—whose eyes see all we do.

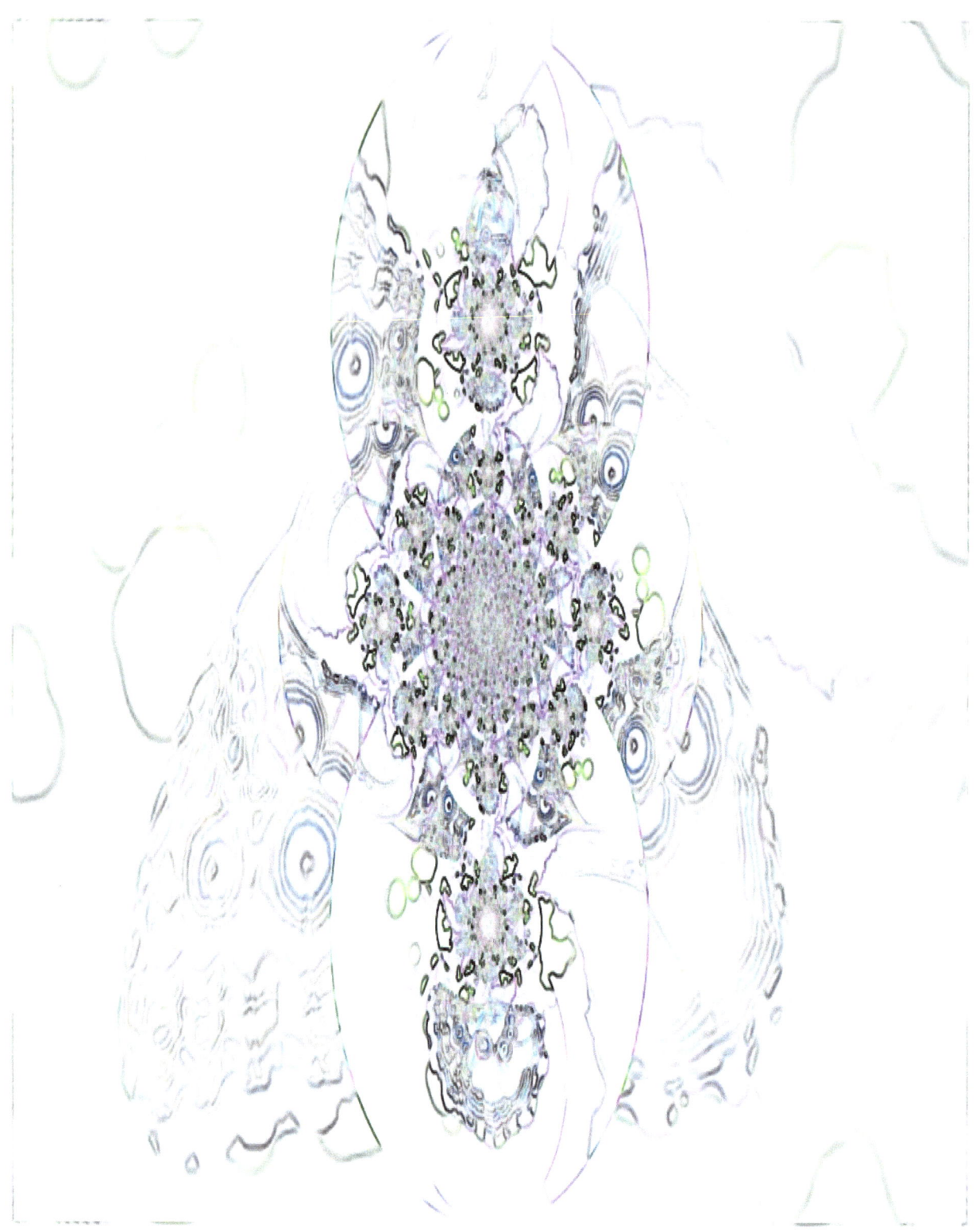

# The Dragon Realm

This is a symbol and artistic piece that was developed into an expressive piece of the inside of the dragon realms. This dragon has a toothy grin and she is waiting to breathe some of her fire into your soul.

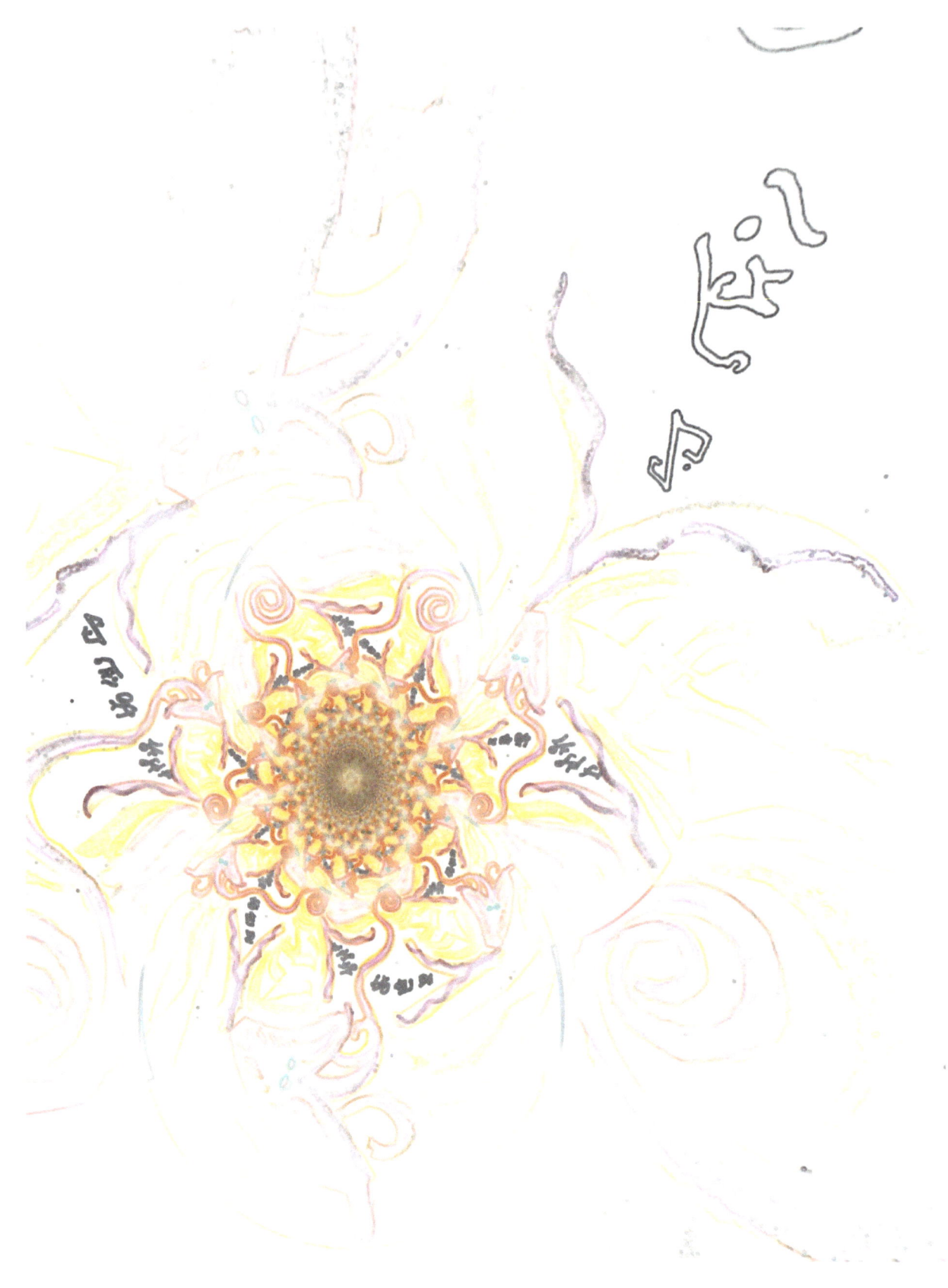

## The Ephiphany

We all get inspiring moments throughout our lifetimes. It is part of the human mind to be inspired, to create and to design our own fate according to these ephiphac moments however for me they were truly spiritual. I have manifested myself through my own ephiphany—I am co-creating and beginning to marvel at all of the intricate miracles available to us all!

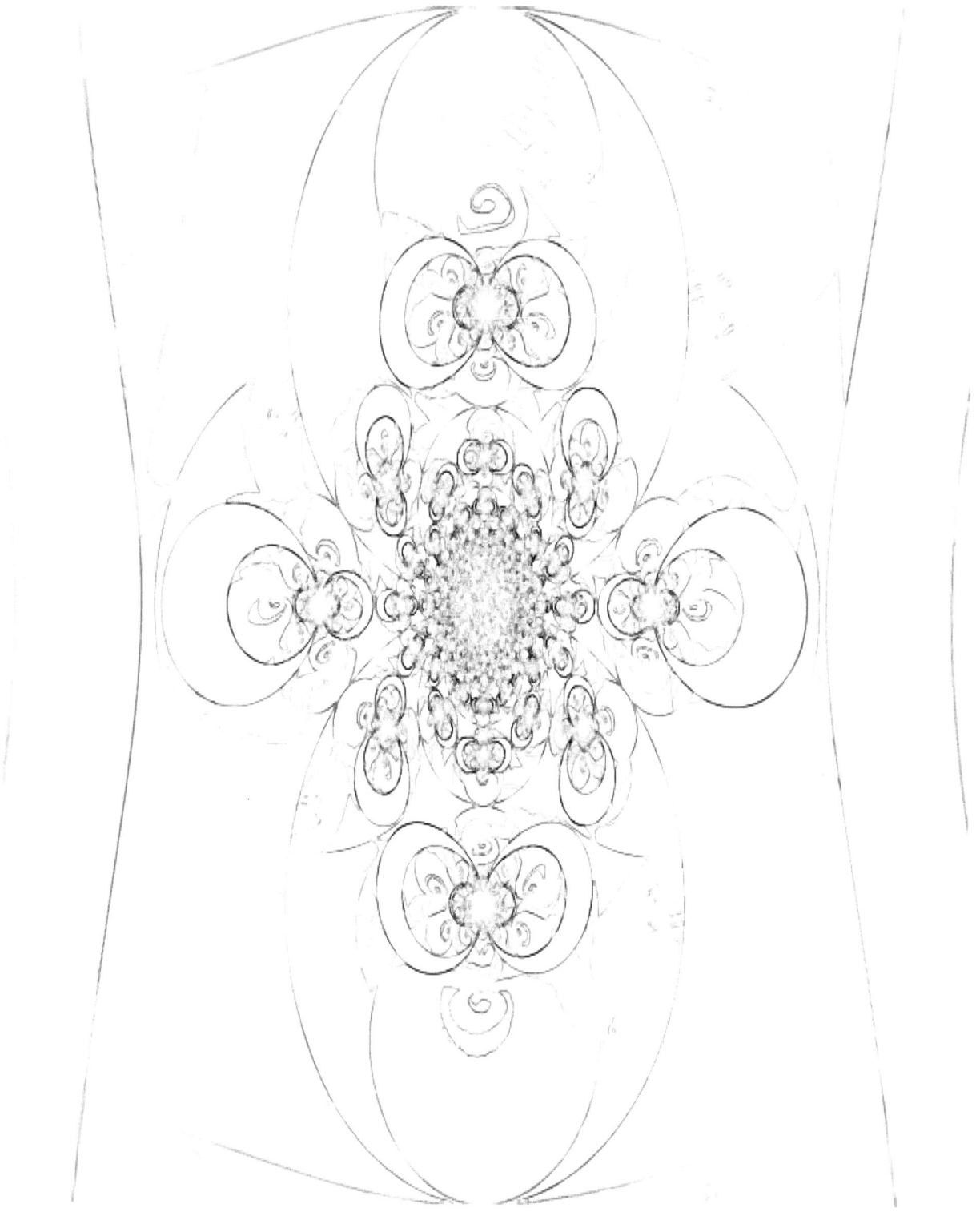

# The Spider

The spider is the keepr of the primoridal alphabet. It is important to teach children when young to respect them and give them distance and honor as an ancient and perhaps not so beloved creature. Their beauty they give to us often goes unappreicated in the intricate webs that they design. The Spider is eternal—and she watches with many eyes.

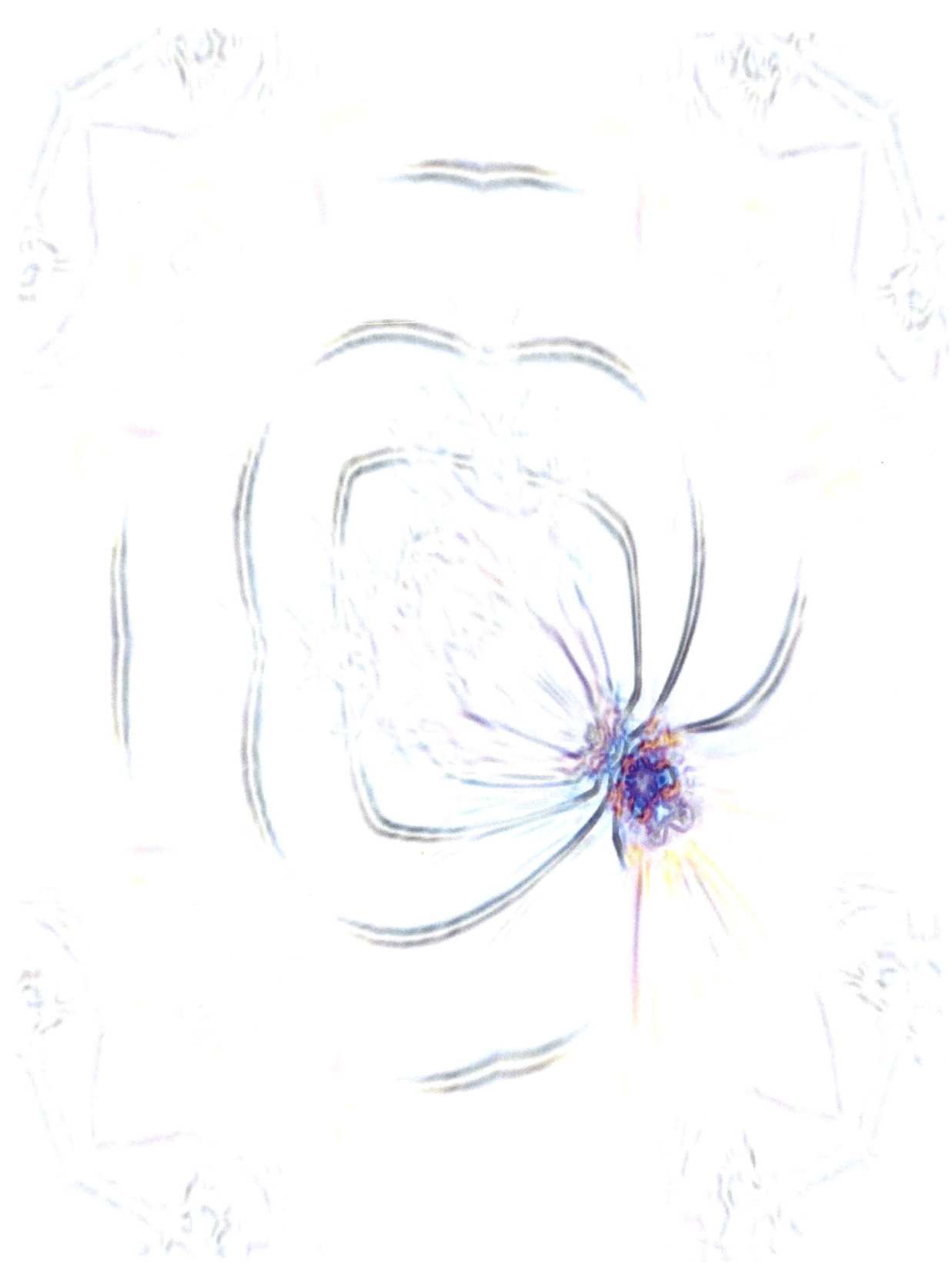

# Neferi

This is a Divine Being that was introduced to me in dreams. She is a wanderer of realms; a protector of souls. She gathers armies under her wings and she soars like an Eagle in flight—she is Neferi-The Eagle Tamer and a Light Seeker and Truth Sayer. She is the Medicine of the Lotus.

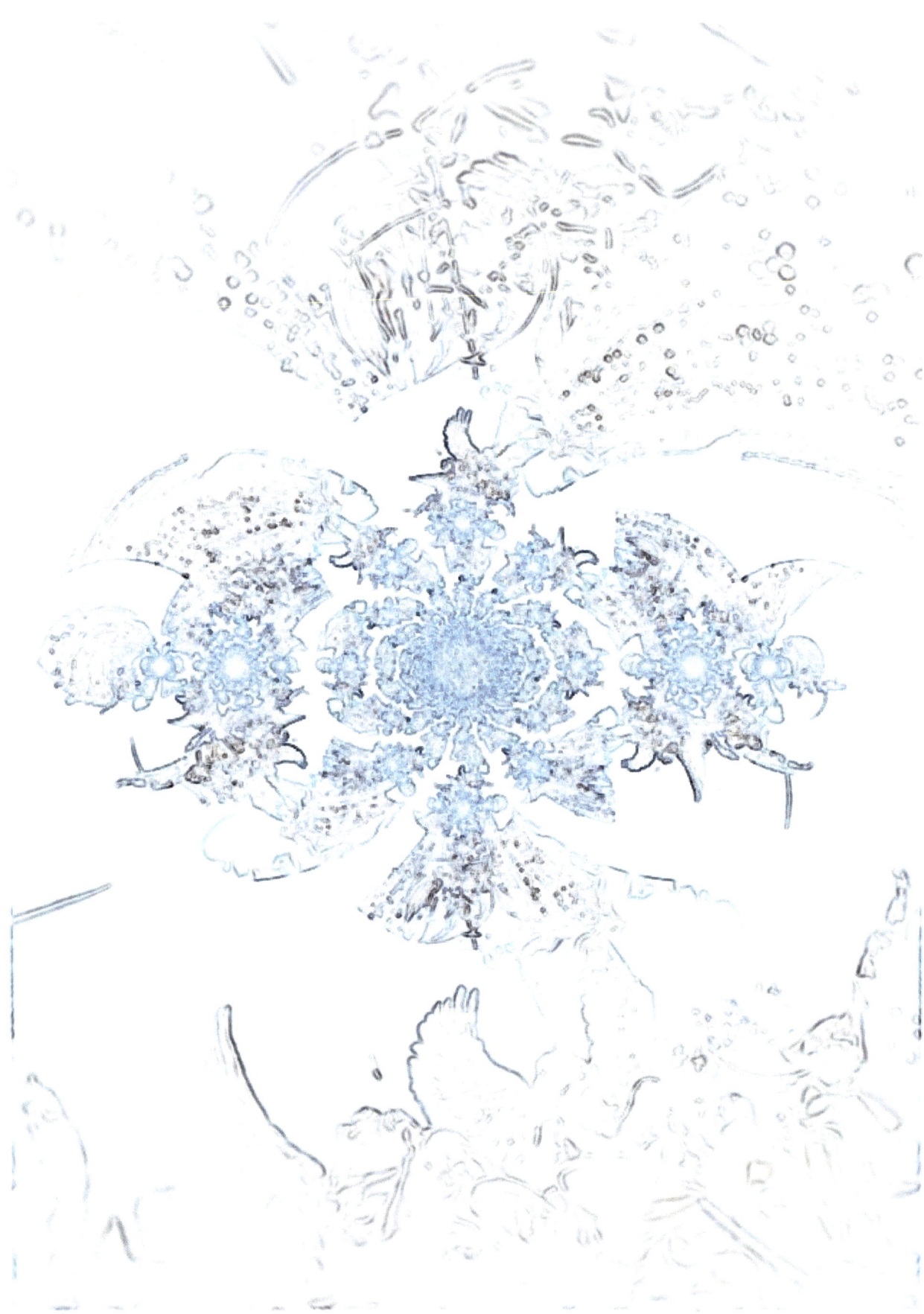

# The Lady of Shalot

She was the Lady of Shalott. She looks sad still-you can see it in her eyes. She longed to be with her one true love—but it was never meant to be. Sir Lancelot she nursed him back to health, and loved him deeply. He did not feel the same and when he left her careand after ten days of grappling over the heavy loss the Lady died of  heart break. She was set into a boat and sent adrift; where Arthurs court found her—Lancelot was given the news and he paid for her funeral. She was the Lady of Shalott.

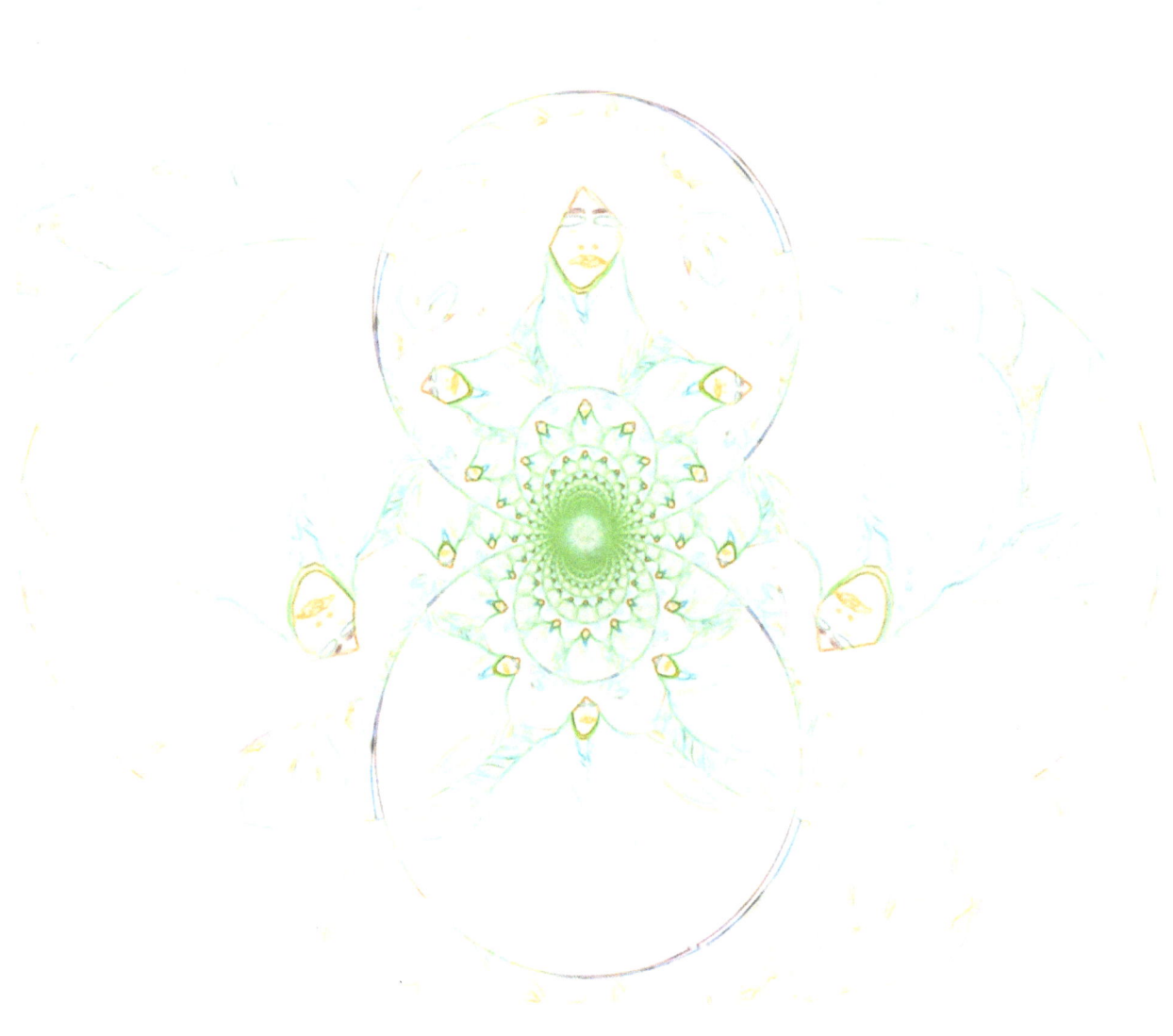

# Peacock Feathers & Turquoise

Jewelry and Feathers have been worn by women and men for eons. To those who study totems this is a symbol of beauty but also bird wisdom. It also is a connection to our past lives and our ancient memories. Turquoise was used by Native Americans and other cultures around the world revel in its Earthly beauty and it too conveys great wisdom to the one wearing it.

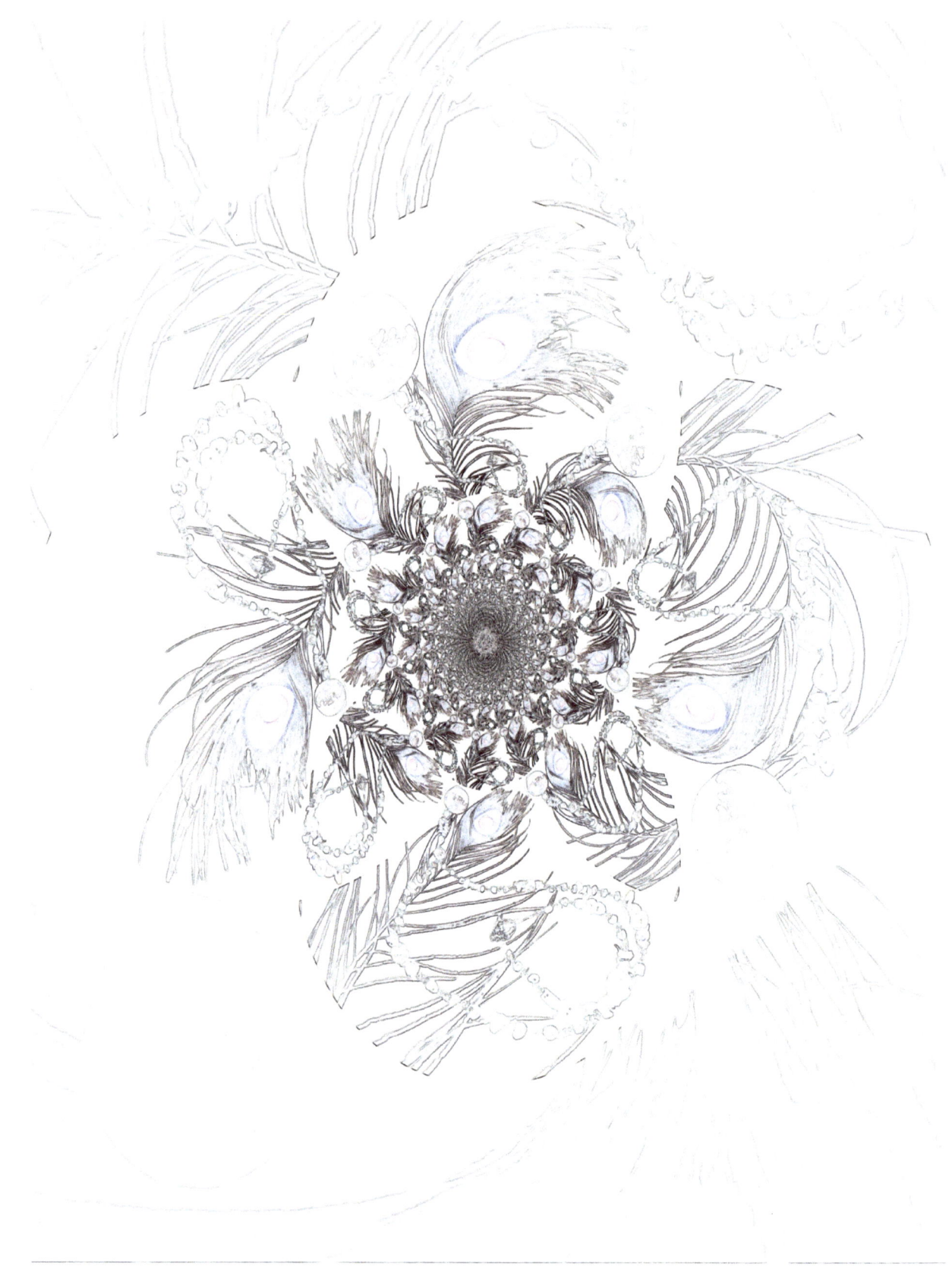

# The Seeker

To all those who feel lost in the dark—do not despair. This symbol is for the faithful and the strong. Let it be a reminder that the light shall guide you home. Whether you are a Christian or not—this is for those who seek the light in the darkness, search for water in the desert or a path in the wilderness. Let this symbol ignite that spark in your mystics heart. Be the seeker, be the querist, and find the answers.

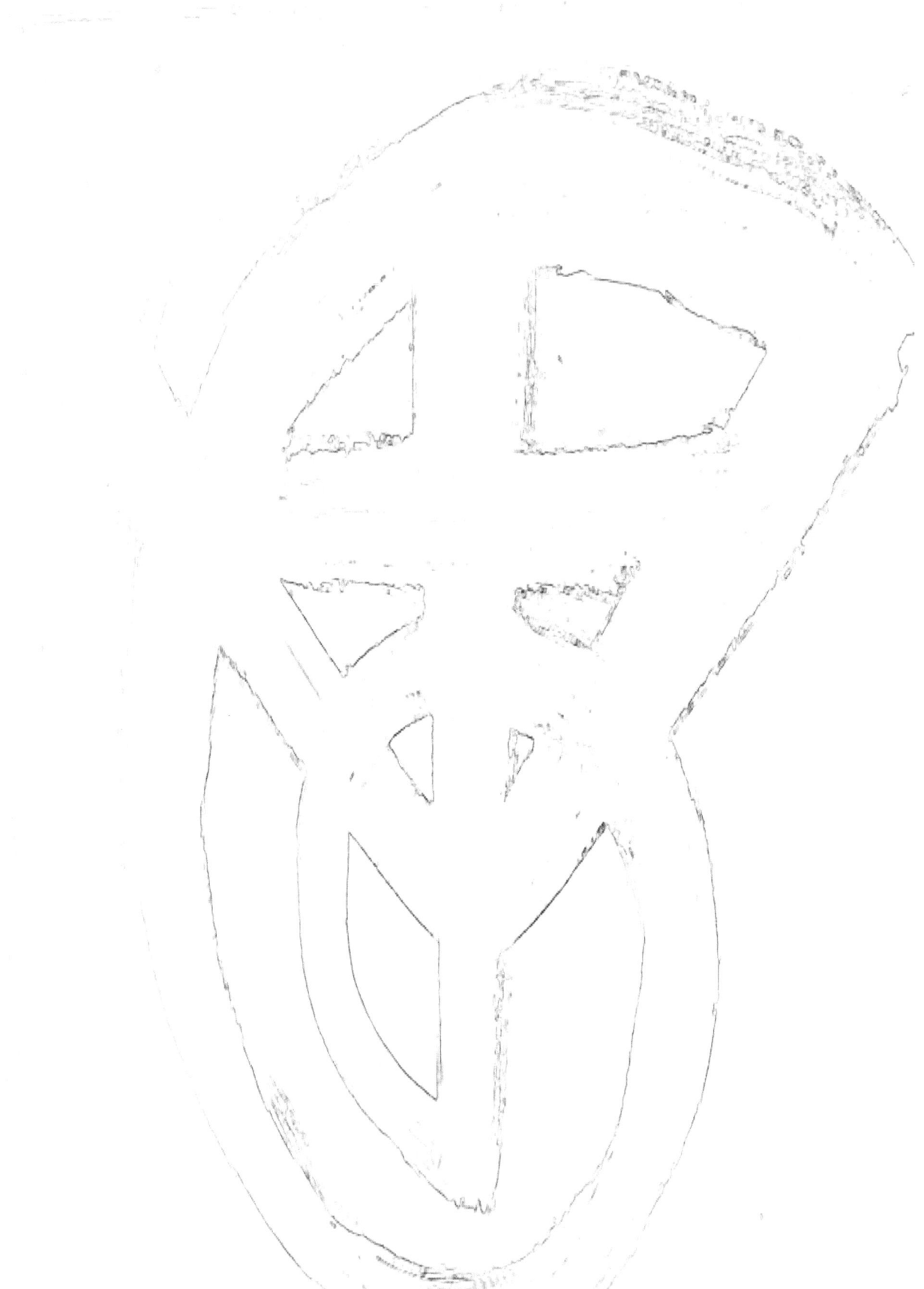

# The Buddha

The Buddha is compassionate, and a reminder that the obstacle is the path. To be peaceful, in harmony with all life and to be considerate and respectful to all things great or small—is but one aspect of the Buddhic nature. The Buddhas reside on the Buddhic Planes and they are a reminder to us that we can strive for an enlightened mind and a loving heart.

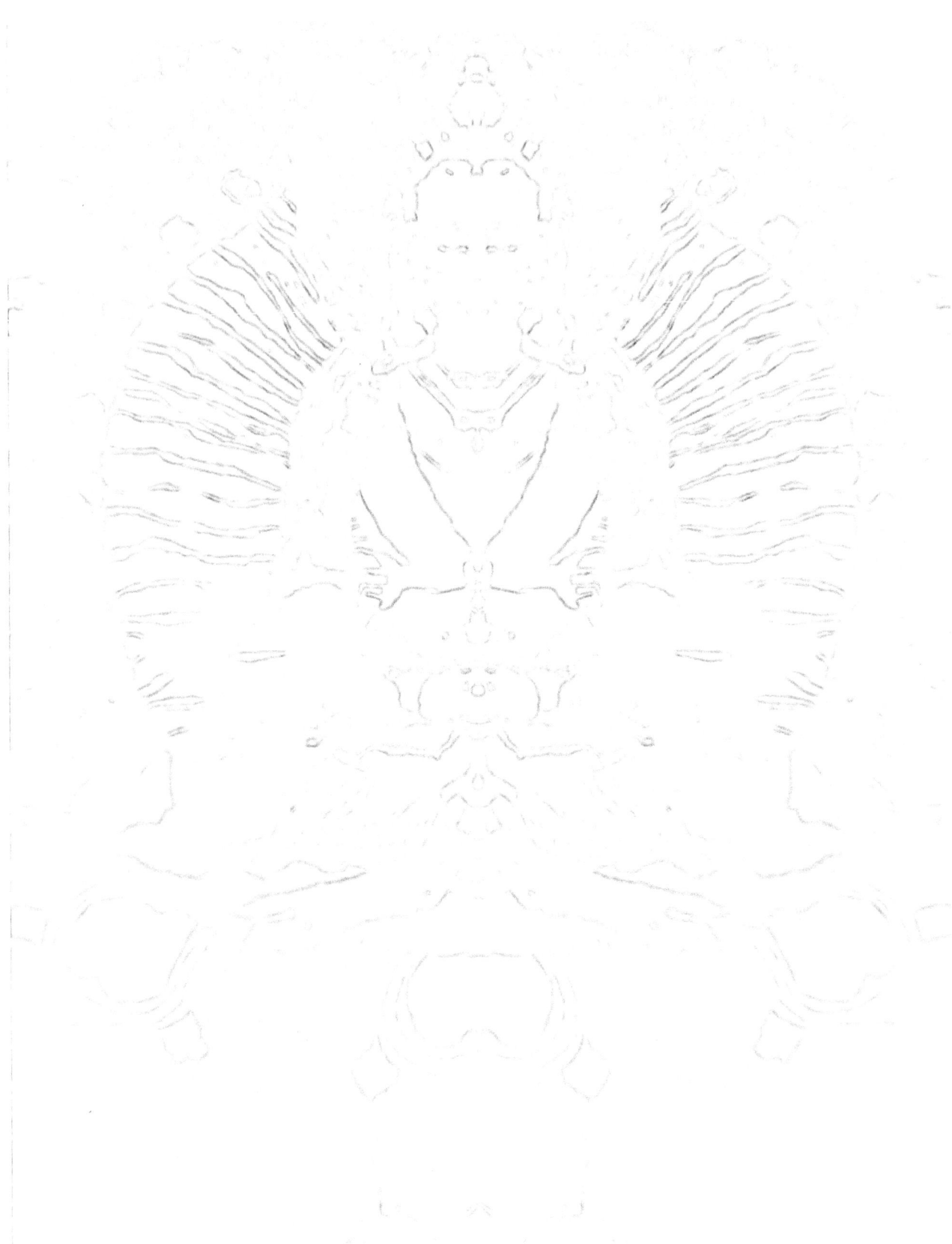

## The Lion Codes

Lions stand for courage, truth and striving for ones highest potential. The lion also represents feminine power, creativity, and ancient magick. The lions hold the keys to the inner kingdom of our souls and they speak only words of Truth to the Seeker. The Lion and the Lamb will one day lie down next to each other without any threat of harm coming to the lamb. Enter the Lion Codes.

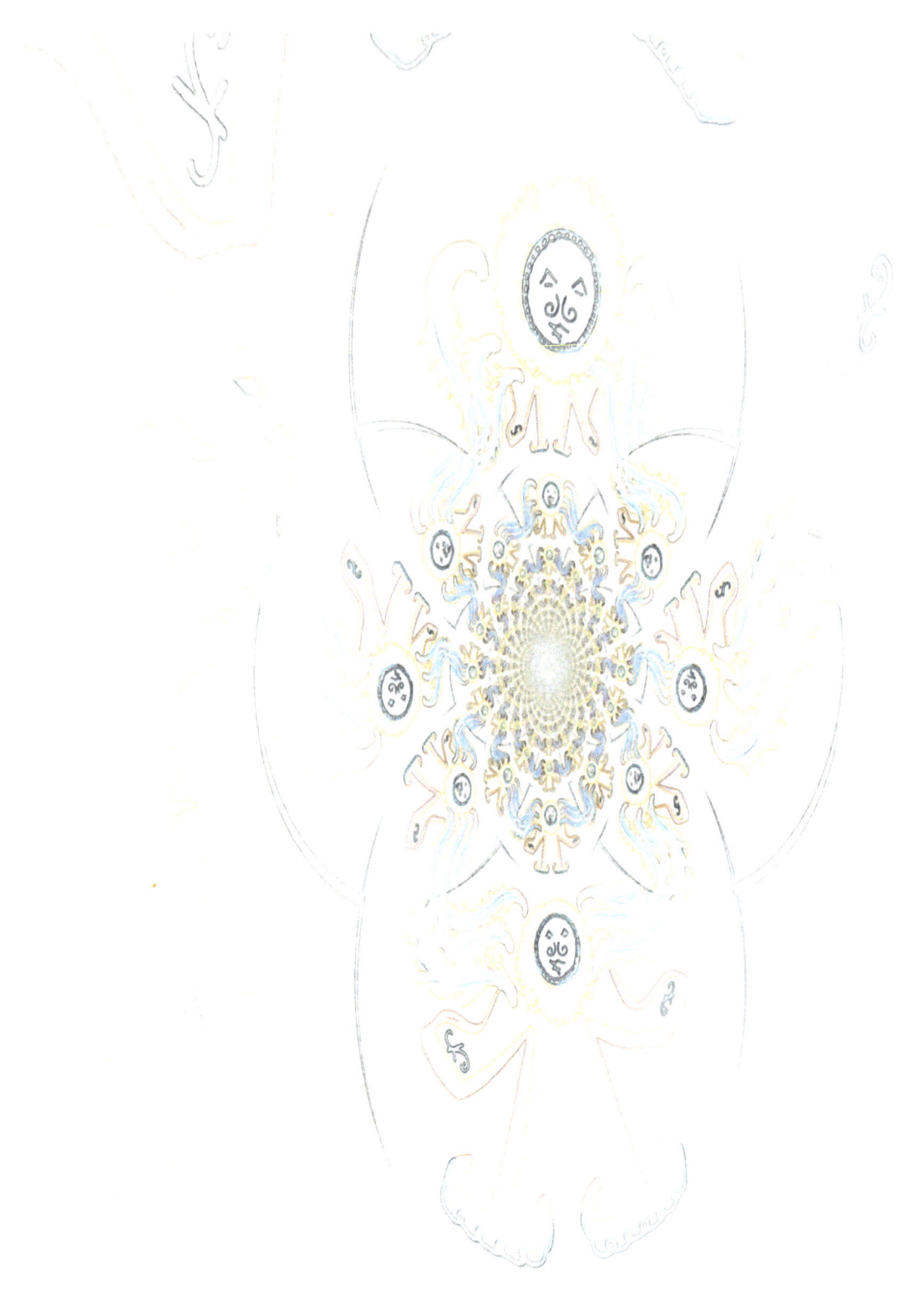

## The Elements

This represents the Five elements: Earth, Fire water Air and Ether or Spirit. The many aspects that lie hidden in the elemental realm are not anything to fear. They are what make up an intrinsic systems of beautious threads of connections. Life, Death, Rebirth and the process of the continum of nature is the elements that we are exposed to on a daily basis. This is also the cover; Jenny Atwell's edit and loving contribution to this project.

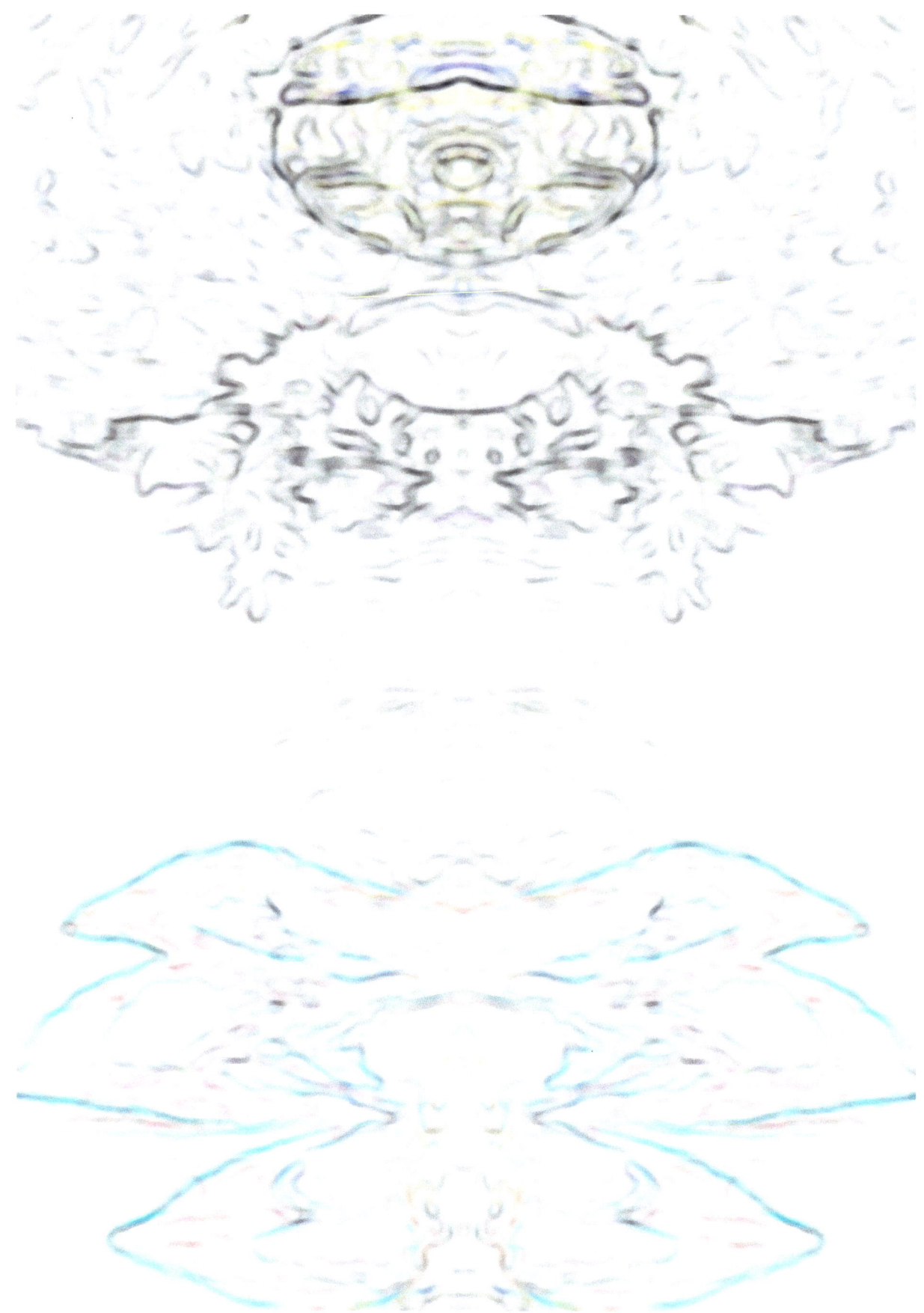

# The Orchid

The Orchid is a flower of intense passion. It is for those who are ignoring their inner desires and sensual side of themselves. They come in many colors and they offer healing for those who are struggling with some aspect of their sexuality. The colors of your desires are like the many shades of Orchids. Ignite your passions as you color this flower.

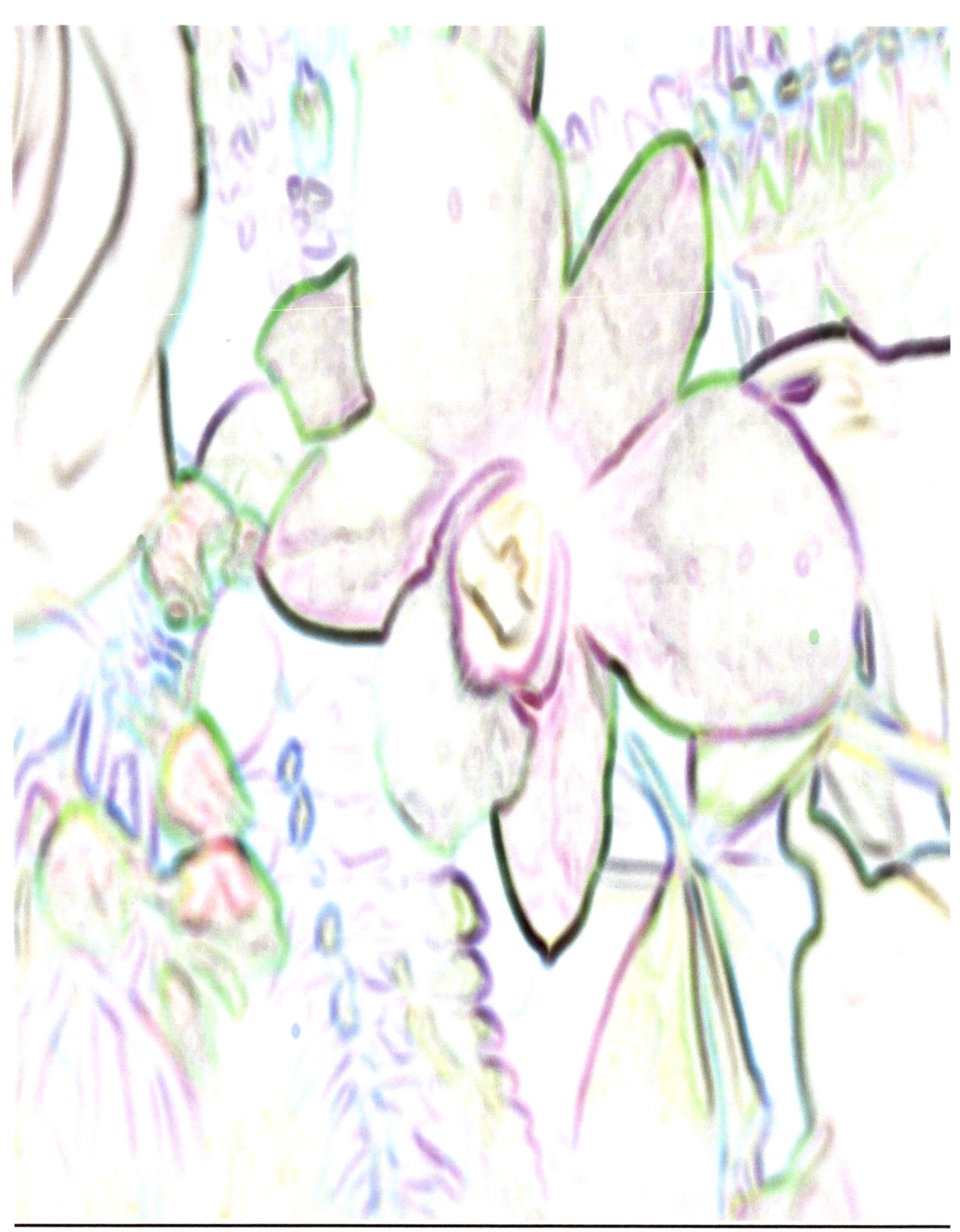

# Summer Time

You know the feeling when you were a little child; swinging on a tire or a regular swing, the wind in your hair. Dusk: frogs croaking, birds twittering in the trees, as the sun sets you are smiling happy and in a perfect place called: Summer time. You may have had a swing in your own backyard; or you went to a park to swing—but the freedom that came with the swiftness of your little legs pumping in the air—with that came the wind in your hair.

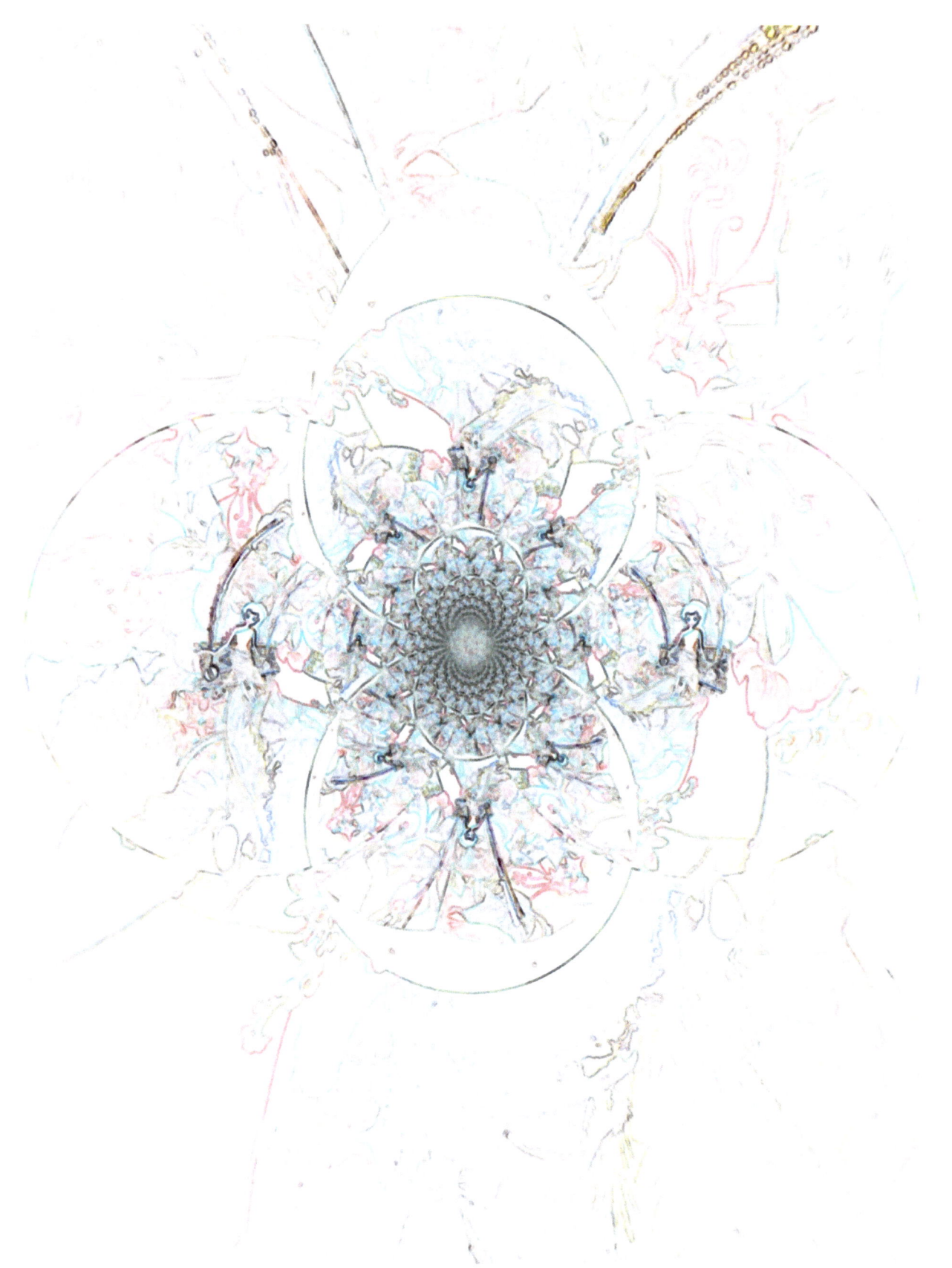

# The Eye

The eye is more than a body part. It is a symbol of knowledge, and second sight. It is the sign for those to know that we are always under the eye of the Universe. We should not fear this though—for we all need inner and outer vision. The Eye is to remind us of all that is seen and unseen in the mystical and also in the logical world. Our eyes are the windows to the soul.

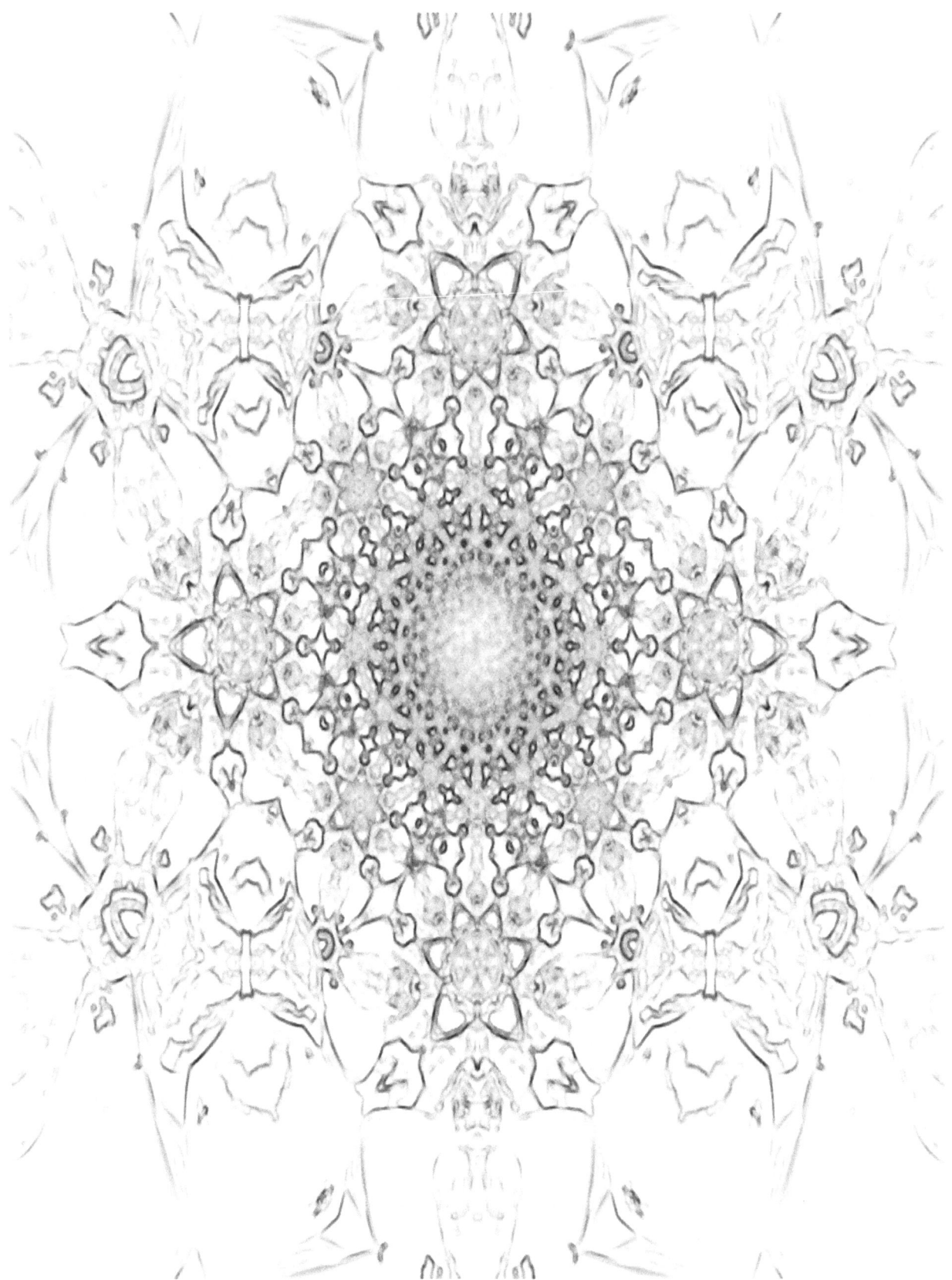

# The Warrior

She is a modern day Joan of Arc—a silent warrior who is content that the time is now not to fight. The battles that wore her soul down are from yesterday. She ponders her next move in this life. She is grateful for the wounds on her soul as she knows she is one of the ancient warriors who wait for the call; for now there is peace—she waits to be summoned but honor is hers. She is guided, guarded and no longer frail. She is the warrior.

# The Artist

She is an artist of her own making. She paints what her heart sees. She designs the tapestry that is woven and colorful webs are spun from her heart strings. She is comfortable in her own skin—the arts are her domain. Like Athena she is content baring the artistry of her heritage and of all her lifetimes. She is an artist who does not fear failure for everything can be altered and changed and brought back into a perfect design.

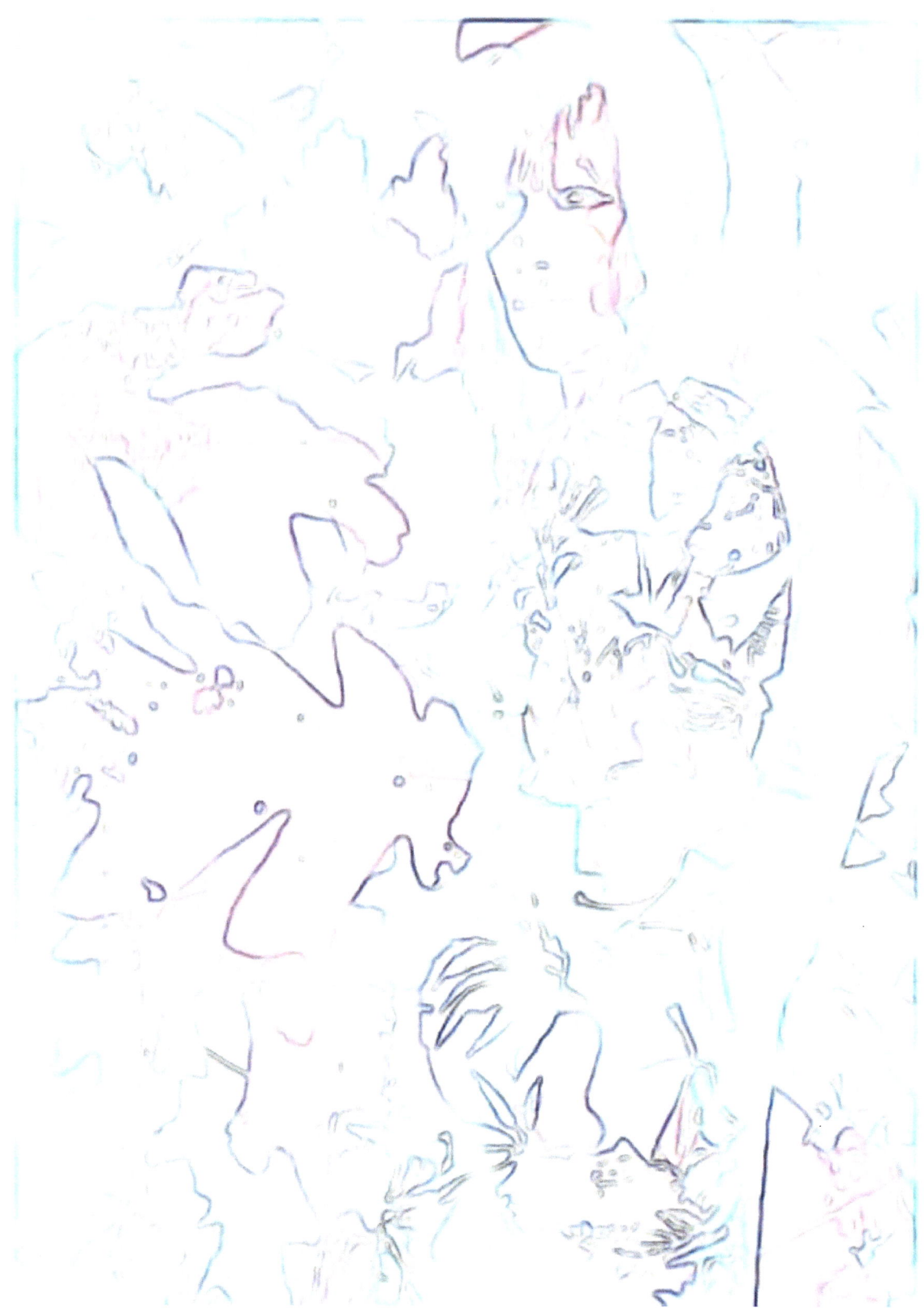

## Biography of Chantal Cash; CH & RMT

I was born in Minnesota and has lived there much of my life. My mother was from the Netherlands, and my father's side, though American, were from Bavaria and Wales. As a child I suffered several traumas. When I was small I was always interested in fairies and Angels. I was always looking for ways to fix things without going to the doctor and I worked with many aspects of myself.

Being the single mother of four children, I was ready to take out a new lease on life. I began looking into all avenues of natural healing. I was sick and tired of being 'sick and tired'. I was in a pre-obese state, I had Hashimoto Thyroiditis. I was angry and was in need of a life changing experience. So I began by taking vitamins, supplements and changing my eating habits. My biggest problem back then was my weight. So I began looking into fast and easy remedies. The one that really helped me was Hypnosis. This though, did not satisfy my curiosity. I then decided to become a Hypnotist.

I took Cal Banyans 5 Path program and became a Certified Hypnotist. I also am a 7th Path Instructor which is the Self-Hypnosis program he teaches, and this was first and foremost the starting point for me. This is what kept me hooked to my weight loss. Hypnosis took me personally and professionally into a new direction. By this time having gotten my physical and emotional health in order, I then moved onto spirit.

By the time I was 32 I knew about love and kindness, but it took a lot of rough patches to feel how far I had really gotten in this life. I saw that compassion moved mountains in my life and that of others. I began to look for ways to change my Spiritual health. I had been raised Catholic and I had been exposed to varying religions over the years; I began to pursue alternatives to Religion.

To be honest, it was hard for me to believe and I never took things at face value. I started to meditate, work with stones and essential oils, I took up a daily prayer practice. This of course eventually put me in the path of Reiki. Since I wanted a true relationship with Source, I started to do research in the different types of energy healing. I started by receiving Reiki from Stephani Brail. I then went on to look at various teachers. I found Shaman Maggie Wahls and took her classes: Level One and Two: Usui Reiki and her Shamanism classes.

Later on, I then took classes from a local instructor Jodi Tschida to receive my Usui Reiki Master and Teacher levels. It did not take long and I found that I was waking up one day to discover that I could do things I never used to be able to do. I woke up one morning after just starting to read a book on Crystals and Minerals. The next morning, after reading only two or three chapters, I knew (inspiringly) all about the stones.

I then began to take other classes introducing myself to Aromatherapy and eventually taking a class to become an Essential Oil Raindrop Specialist. I began practicing telepathy. I began to communicate with spirits and see peoples past lives imprinted on them. I established a relationship with my guides and Angels, and eventually it led me to communication with the Divine or Source as I prefer to say.

For the first time I really began to see LIFE for the wonder it really was. All areas of Natural Medicine had been put into my path. I was eager to learn and applied myself where I thought I could be of the most help. Other areas of interest I have acquired and incorporated into my business are: Crystal stone Layouts, Dowsing and Reiki; classes and sessions, Tarot readings and Oracle readings, Jewelry making and other crafts, to name just a few.

In my spare time I write poetry and other literary works, make scrap books, garden, I read and do research for my work. I have four children: two daughters and two sons. My sons have Autism. I am a support manager for a Non-profit company that enables disabled people to lead more independent lives. I work with my sons and have worked with other Autistic children and Adults. I find this work to be extremely rewarding. I enjoy my job very much.

In addition, I have four businesses. I have created these businesses as a way of reaching out to people in these varying avenues of interest. I also am working on finishing my Associates in Criminal Justice, though that has been placed on the back burner for now. I would like to do non-Profit work as an Advocate to serve those who experience social injustice. Specifically: focusing in the areas of the develop mentally disabled; and to continue my work with Autistic persons. In any of my sessions my focus is Mind body Spirit connection. In any of my businesses I utilize all my tools and I use any knowledge I have to help my family, my clients, friends, and community.

New Perceptions Hypnosis & Reiki is my first business that I opened in 2007. I then incorporated the Reiki into my first business as well. Inner Chi Crystal Jewelry and Chi KI Arts & Crafts are catered around spiritually made gifts and other handmade items.

In addition, I have MAOM: this is an acronym for Metaphysical Association of Minnesota. This business focuses on people who are having spiritual issues or are in need of guidance due to a haunting, spiritual attack or other supernatural occurrence. I specialize in assisting people to invoke a higher spiritual awareness and when necessary I do spirit re-leasement therapy known as SRT through Hypnosis or I make house calls to assist the client in removing and cleansing property, the people that live there and their pets.

The aspect about the work that I love the most is reaching out to people and assisting them in their goals towards health and healing, be it: Emotional, Physical or Spiritual. Working with Source daily helps me to be creative in all areas of my life. I enjoy being a Co-Creator with Source. I work with The Earth, the elements, the Universe, the all in all. I am excited to teach people about Reiki and Self-Hypnosis and to help them learn how to explore their past, to embrace their present and look forward to their future.

In addition I have been writing for many years. Specifically, short stories, fiction, poetry and of course self- help/self- trans-formation informative guiding works. I am  the author of the book on Dowsing, Totems , Reiki and much more. I am interested in many metaphysical topics: and write about those varying issues and topics that people come to me for through teaching Hypnosis or Reiki—my interests are many and truly are not limited. I enjoy writing in my spare time and it has become very important to me to write daily. I feel that the negative experiences from my childhood helped to transform me into the person that I am today. I believe that knowing what I know now, we can transform or worries, our fears and even our traumas into something positive.

Art is just one way to get in touch with the deepest parts of the human soul. I have found that as I grow lighter and become a happier human being I create better, more thoughtful art and it is my joy to share with the world; just a little piece of my souls evolution and growth—remember that if I can do it; you can too!